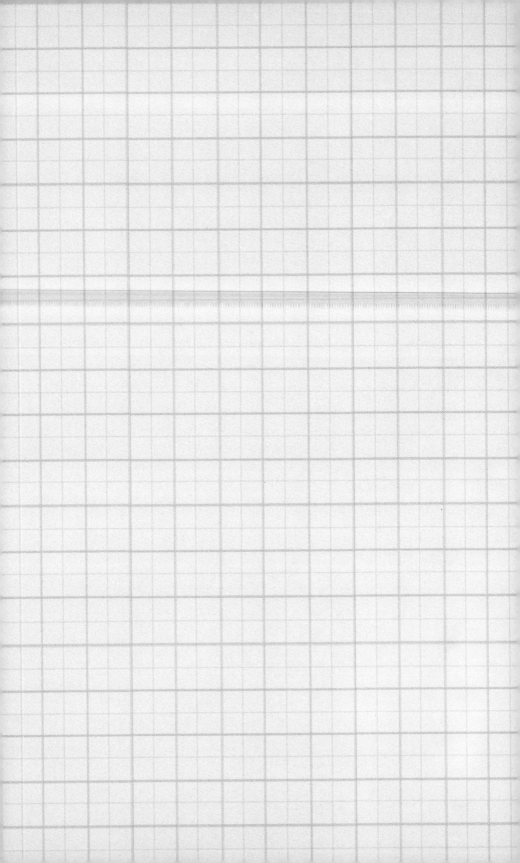

ADA TWIST, SCIENTIST
THE WHY FILES

TEAM GREEN!

By Andrea Beaty and Dr. Theanne Griffith

Amulet Books • New York

To Dr. Theanne Griffith with many, many thanks — A.B.

For Asha, my future coauthor — T.G.

Library of Congress Control Number 2024936210

ISBN 978-1-4197-7044-9

ADA TWIST ™ Netflix. Used with permission.
Story and text © 2024 Andrea Beaty
ADA TWIST series imagery © Netflix, Inc. and used with permission from Netflix.

Ada Twist, Scientist and the Questioneers created by Andrea Beaty and David Roberts

Book design by Charice Silverman

Illustrations by Steph Stilwell

Images courtesy Shutterstock.com: **Page 2:** Plastic glass used for drinking water in a bin - Environmental problem concept / Non-compostable waste, wk1003mike. **Page 3:** portrait of daughter and mother frying mushrooms on the stove together for dinner at the kitchen, AT Production. **Page 6:** Transportation of oil and natural gas by truck in Oil Refinery factory and petrochemical plant – Petroleum industry, tonton. **Page 12:** The white tour boat Mariefred, a steam ship taking off for a guided tour with tourists, Magnus Binnerstam; Boiling water with steam in a pot on an electric stove in the kitchen. Blurred background, selective focus, Viktoria Kytt. **Page 18:** Dead and Shriveled Spathiphyllum Plant in Plant Pot Isolated on white, Bob Mawby. **Page 23:** Side wind blowing happy and smiling asian's girl hair in a spring cold day, selective focus on the hair in front of the girl's face, Chalermpon Poungpeth. **Page 27:** Child in swimming pool. Having fun on vacation at the hotel pool. Colorful vacation concept, Igor Link; hot fry egg on pavement, Holly Vegter. **Page 34:** hydroelectric station with tidal turbines in the current, Breedfoto. **Page 35:** tidal current powers the water turbines, Breedfoto; Happy baby boy and girl – young surfers ride with fun on one surfboard. Active family lifestyle, kids outdoor water sport lessons, swimming activity in surf camp. Sea beach summer holiday with child, Denis Moskvinov. **Page 44:** Throw children's toys in the trash. A gloved hand pulls a toy car out of a garbage can, Svetliy. **Page 46:** Trash that is a piece of cloth, old cloth is thrown away along the way. Waste that is difficult to degrade And cause pollution, neenawat khenyothaa; Teddy bear thrown in the trash like garbage, Irina Kozorog. **Page 49:** plastic bottle garbage for recycling concept reuse, ITTIGallery. **Page 50:** Worker sorts trash on conveyor belt at waste recycling plant, Nordroden. **Page 51:** Heap of old metal and equipment for recycling, sima. **Page 62:** Africa American biotechnologist holding young butterhead for research with other species vegetables in organic farm. Good quality products. Remember growing plant. Earths day concept, Manop Boonpeng. **Page 63:** Female geologist using laptop computer examining nature, analyzing rocks or pebbles. Researchers collect samples of biological materials. Environmental and ecology research, Pornpimon Ainkaew. Images courtesy Public Domain: **Page 9:** Clouds of smoke around the 323rd Delta rocket on launch pad 17B, NASA/Jerry Cannon. **Page 24:** The Sun by the Atmospheric Imaging Assembly of NASA's Solar Dynamics Observatory - 20100819, NASA. **Page 38:** NesjavellirPowerPlant edit2, Gretar Ívarsson. **Page 42:** Power County Wind Farm 003, ENERGY.GOV. **Page 51:** Cube of compressed paper at Berkeley recycling center 1, D Coetzee. **Page 65:** Lisa P. Jackson official portrait, Eric Vance. Images courtesy Creative Commons: **Page 3:** Panasonic AIR CONDITIONER OUTDOOR UNIT & MITSUBISHI ELECTRIC WINDOW TYPE AIR CONDITIONER OUTDOOR UNIT, Dinkun Chen (CC BY-SA 4.0). **Page 5:** Sun rise from above the skies, ozma (CC BY 2.0). **Page 6:** Coal Hill, Bernhard Hanakam (CC BY-SA 3.0). **Page 7:** Klövbergets naturreservat, trees between cliffs and water, Krr005 (CC BY-SA 4.0). **Page 8:** city of lights, paul bica (CC BY 2.0). **Page 9:** JET BLUE A320 (2705213018), JET BLUE A320 (CC BY-SA 2.0). **Page 10:** Heavy traffic rajchadamri road, Boonlert Aroonpiboon (CC BY-SA 4.0). **Page 11:** Filling the gas tank, OregonDOT (CC BY 2.0). **Page 13:** Cart full of bituminous coal, Jacek Rużyczka (CC BY-SA 4.0). **Page 19:** Drought land dry mud BOUHANIFIA Algeria, Hydrosami (CC BY-SA 4.0). **Page 22:** Rushing of Water (Snake River) (50595967667), G. Lamar (CC BY 2.0). **Page 24:** Leaves Do Cartwheels, David Goehring (CC by 2.0). **Page 25:** Rushing Water and Autumn Leaves (19219470896), Eric Kilby (CC BY-SA 2.0); Castle Geyser erupting, G. Edward Hohnson (CC BY 3.0). **Page 26:** Hallig Hooge, Germany, view from the Backenswarft, Michael Gäbler (CC BY 3.0). **Page 28:** Solar panels on house roof, Gray Watson (CC BY-SA 3.0). **Page 30:** Windmills of Consuegra (7079301881), Michal Osmenda (CC BY 2.0); Whole wheat grain flour being scooped, Margaret Hoogstrate, (CC BY 3.0); Home made sour dough bread, Tomascastelazo (CC BY-SA 4.0). **Page 31:** Wind Power Kamisu 08, Σ64 (CC BY 3.0). **Page 32:** Windmill blade, TheMuuj (CC BY 2.0); Haldenstein - Calandawind Rotor, Kecko (CC BY 2.0). **Page 36:** Fimmvorduhals 2010 03 27 dawn, Boaworm (CC BY 4.0). **Page 37:** Castle Geyser erupting, G. Edward Hohnson (CC BY 3.0). **Page 38:** Krafla geothermal power station wiki, Ásgeir Eggertsson (CC BY-SA 3.0). **Page 43:** Female house sparrow at Kodai, Deepak Sundar (CC BY-SA 4.0); Grey headed flying fox - AndrewMercer IMG41848, Andrew Mercer (CC BY-SA 4.0). **Page 48:** Recycling bin New Orleans 2007, Bart Everson (CC BY 2.0). **Page 52:** Row of trash cans, East Hollywood, Downtowngal (CC BY-SA 4.0). **Page 53:** 30th Av 31st St td (2019-08-21) 06, Tdorante10 (CC BY-SA 4.0). **Page 63:** Beaches of Alexandria clean up in 2017, photo by Hatem Moushir 22, Hatem Moushir (CC BY-SA 4.0). **Page 64:** Wangari Maathai, Oregon State University (CC BY-SA 2.0). **Page 65:** Dorceta Taylor, Peggy Shepard, Bunyan Bryant and Paul Mohai, University of Michigan School for Environment and Sustainability (CC BY 2.0)

ABRAMS The Art of Books
195 Broadway, New York, NY 10007
abramsbooks.com

MIX
Paper | Supporting responsible forestry
FSC® C144853

My brother, Arthur, played
in a tennis tournament. The
players got very hot and
very thirsty. They all drank
water from plastic cups,
which they threw away. It
was A LOT of cups.

1

But that doesn't seem very sustainable! If everyone throws cups away now, will there be any cups left in the future? What will happen to the planet if everyone is throwing plastic away?

It's a mystery! A riddle! A puzzle! A quest!

Time to find out what sustainability is about!

Our planet is filled with living and nonliving things. We get the energy to make food, to heat or cool our homes, and even to make books (like this one!) from nonliving things called **natural resources**.

Where do books come from?

Natural gas, metals, oil, coal, air, and sunlight are all examples of natural resources.

Different places can have more or less of a natural resource depending on their environments. Some of these resources can be replaced, while other resources cannot.

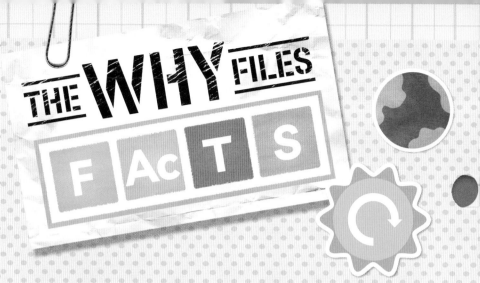

THE WHY FILES

FACTS

- A **RENEWABLE** natural resource can be used and replaced naturally. Sunlight and air are renewable resources.

- A **NONRENEWABLE** natural resource cannot be replaced by nature. Once a nonrenewable resource is used up, there isn't more available for the future. Coal and oil are nonrenewable resources.

- Most natural resources are nonrenewable and will eventually run out as we keep using them.

- **SUSTAINABILITY** is the practice of caring for these resources so all living things can benefit from them now and in the future. This is also called **CONSERVATION**.

Fascinating!

One of the main uses of natural resources is to make energy. We need energy to power our homes, drive cars, fly planes, launch rockets, and make just about any object you can think of.

Natural resources create energy as they are changed from one form to another. For example, when we put gasoline into a car, it is a liquid. As we drive the car, the gasoline is heated, and heat changes the fuel from liquid to vapor. This change is called a **reaction**, and it releases the energy that the car uses to drive.

The same change happens when you boil water: It turns into steam. In fact, boats were once powered by the steam created by heating large amounts of water.

Coal is also used for energy. Burning coal gives off heat that is used to boil water and turn it into steam. The energy that is released by turning water into steam can be changed once again into electricity.

About one-fourth of all the electricity used in the United States comes from power plants that burn coal. Coal is a nonrenewable resource.

Remember what that means? After we use it up, there will be no more left on Earth.

The gasoline that powers our cars is made from oil found deep in the ground. That oil is also a nonrenewable resource.

Burning coal and oil to create energy is also bad for our environment. When these substances are burned, they release **greenhouse gases** into the air.

Greenhouse gases like carbon dioxide trap heat in our atmosphere, and by doing so make our planet hotter. This process causes **global warming** and **climate change**.

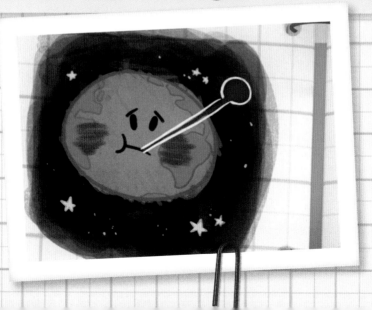

THE GREENHOUSE EFFECT

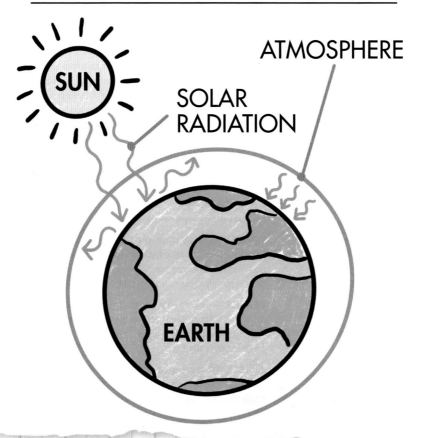

Greenhouse gases get their name from greenhouses, which are clear structures that trap heat from the Sun in order to grow plants year-round.

Our lives rely on the use of coal, oil, and other nonrenewable natural resources for energy and electricity. Eventually, these resources will run out.

Our use of nonrenewable resources is also hurting our planet and the other living things we share it with. Because of global warming, sea levels are rising, we have more floods and droughts, and some wildlife and plants will not be able to survive as our planet gets hotter.

WHAT CAN WE DO?

WE NEED A BRAINSTORM

1. We could go shopping on other planets for resources. We would need a very big shopping cart, though.

2. We could find new energy resources. Like cheese! Or pogo sticks!

3. We could use our existing resources more wisely!

One way that scientists are trying to preserve natural resources and stop climate change is by creating tools that allow us to get energy from renewable resources. Sunlight, wind, moving water, and even heat made by Earth itself are all forms of renewable energy.

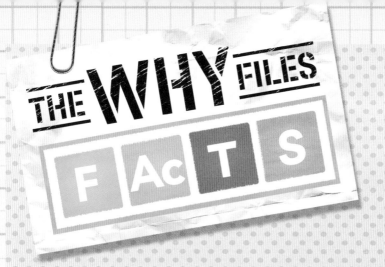

RENEWABLE ENERGY SOURCES

- **SOLAR ENERGY** from the Sun can be changed into electricity.

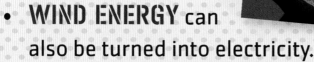

- **WIND ENERGY** can also be turned into electricity.

- **HYDROPOWER** is energy produced by moving water.

- Energy from the heat made by Earth is called **GEOTHERMAL ENERGY.**

The Sun is the ultimate power source. It is full of energy and powers nearly all living things on Earth by providing sunlight. Energy from the Sun is called **solar energy**. Humans have been using solar energy for thousands of years. We have used it to cook food, to keep warm, and to dry clothes.

Sunny-side up!

More recently, scientists have figured out how to turn solar energy into electricity using **solar cells**. Solar cells trap the energy from sunlight and transform that energy into electricity. **Solar panels** are made up of many solar cells.

Humans have also used **wind energy** for hundreds of years. **Windmills** were created to turn wind power into energy that was used to grind up grain. Today we use windmills to create electricity.

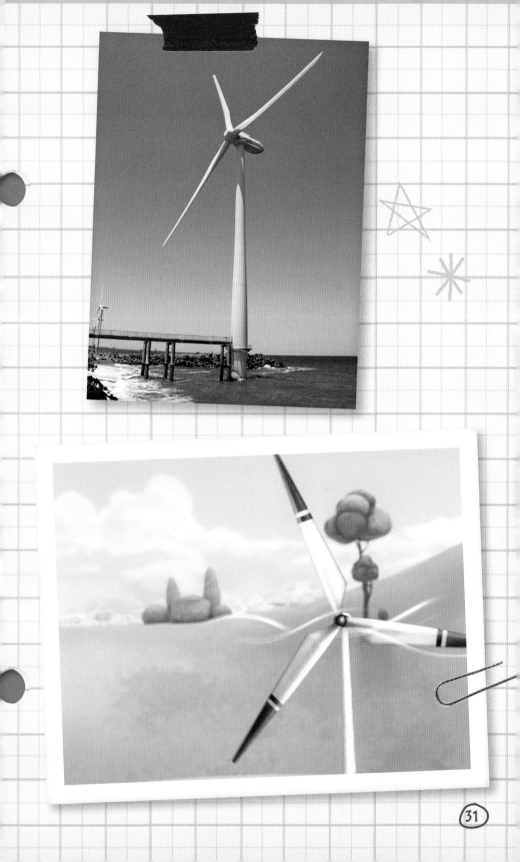

As wind moves the blades on a windmill, a **rotor** inside the windmill spins. The rotor is connected to a **generator**. A generator is a machine that turns the energy from the spinning rotor into electricity.

A rotor is a big spinny thing that moves air or water! Swoooosh!

GENERATOR

BLADES

ROTOR

TOWER

Moving water also creates a force called **hydropower**. **Water turbines** look like upside-down windmills. The underwater blades spin as water flows over them, creating energy that is turned into electricity.

The motion of the ocean!

⟵----

35

Geothermal energy is heat that comes from inside Earth.

The core of Earth is very hot, and that heat has a lot of energy. When a volcano or geyser erupts, it is releasing geothermal energy. Geothermal power plants turn the energy contained in Earth's center into electricity.

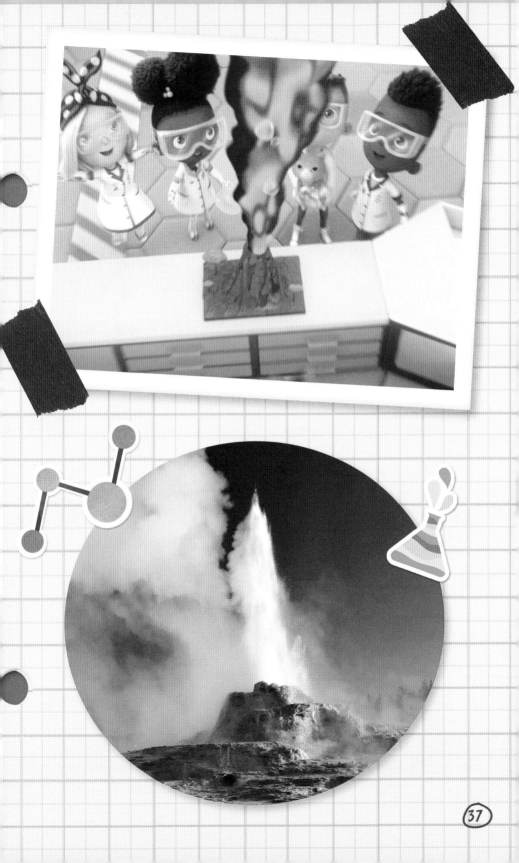

Renewable natural resources are a better source of energy than nonrenewable resources, because they don't make as much pollution, and we don't have to worry about them running out. But getting energy from renewable resources still has some problems.

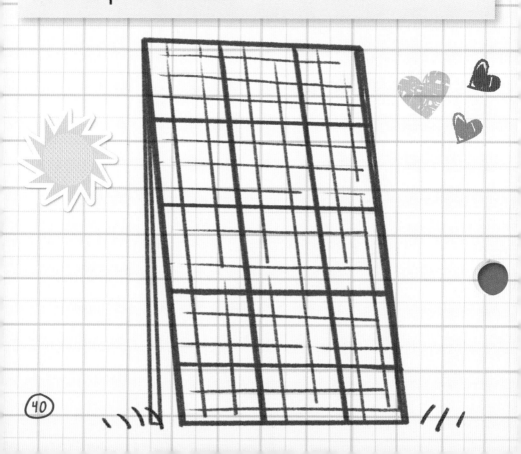

For example, in one day, the average solar panel produces only enough energy to make one plastic water bottle.

A windmill can make enough energy to power about 940 homes in the United States.

Wow!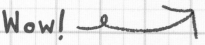

But windmills also harm wild animals. Birds and bats can get hurt if they fly into windmills. Windmills also make a lot of noise that can disturb wildlife, and building windmills takes away habitats from various animals.

If we want to preserve our planet and the resources it gives us, we must do more than change the natural resources we use. We must also use fewer of them.

Waste is anything we throw away. Humans make a lot of waste. We throw away food that we don't eat. We throw away toys that we no longer play with. We also throw away clothes and even electronic devices.

The more things we use, the more we must throw away. And all that trash pollutes our environment and destroys the habitats of other living things we share our planet with.

To create less waste, we must live more sustainably. That means we have to think about the choices we make in almost every part of daily life.

Home

A poem by Ada Twist

I live on a planet that gives
me so much.

Oxygen, energy, water, and
such!

For this I am grateful, and I
want to learn

how to take care of our
Earth in return.

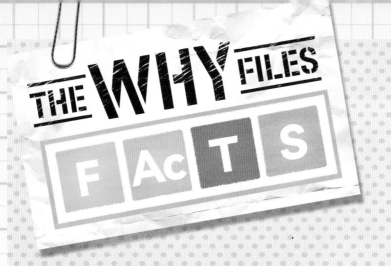

THE THREE Rs OF SUSTAINABILITY

- We can
  RECYCLE
  things instead
  of throwing
  them away.

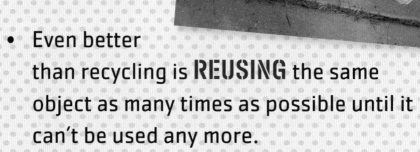

- Even better
  than recycling is **REUSING** the same
  object as many times as possible until it
  can't be used any more.

- The best way to live sustainably is to **REDUCE** the overall number of things we use. The less we use, the less waste we produce, and the more natural resources we can save for the future.

Recycling is changing old products into new ones. After you recycle plastic bottles and metal cans, the items are taken to a recycling plant, where they are remade into the materials for brand-new things. The recycled material could be made into new bottles or cans. It could even be made into things like bikes.

Recycling is better than simply throwing things in the trash. It means we can take fewer resources from Earth.

Recycling plants need energy and electricity to change old items into new ones. This means that recycling also uses natural resources.

Many recycling plants get energy from nonrenewable resources that produce pollution. And almost half of the things that we send to recycling plants cannot be recycled anyway. Eventually, they just end up with the regular trash.

Sometimes this is because the item is too dirty to be recycled. For example, plastic that's covered in food cannot be recycled.

Reusing is a great way to reduce waste and use fewer resources. For example, if you order a toy that comes in a big box, you can reuse that box instead of throwing it away or recycling it. You could use it to store arts and crafts supplies or to organize things in your room.

If you don't like how the box looks, you can decorate it with stickers, doodles, or other stuff that you like! That is a more sustainable choice than buying a new storage box.

Reusable items, like portable water bottles and washable snack bags, are also more sustainable choices than the disposable items you throw away after one use. Reusing something is also called **upcycling**.

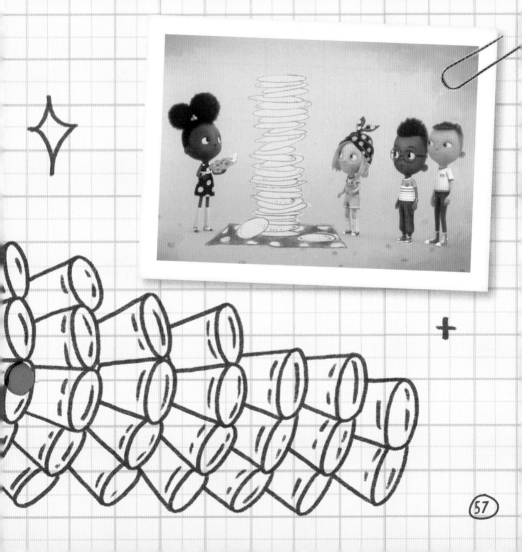

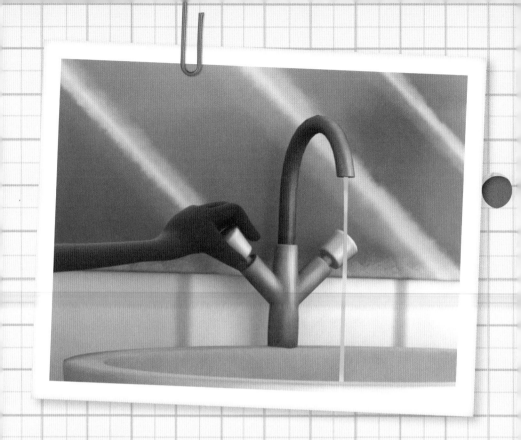

Recycling and reusing are both good ways to live sustainably. But **reducing** the number of things we use is the best way to make less waste and use fewer resources.

Turning off the lights when you're not using them and taking shorter showers are easy ways you can reduce the resources you use every day. Another great way to reduce what you use is to buy only what you need.

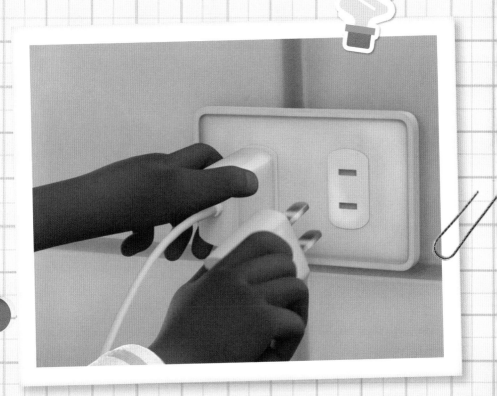

When making choices about what to buy, try asking yourself: *Is this something I need or something I want?* Remember, the less we buy, the less we throw away. And the less we throw away, the healthier our planet becomes.

People have been working for a long time to help figure out ways for us to live more sustainably, use fewer natural resources, and conserve the environment so it can be used by all living things. These people are called **environmentalists** or **conservationists**.

Environmentalists and conservationists work to protect the air, water, animals, plants, and other natural resources from harm caused by humans.

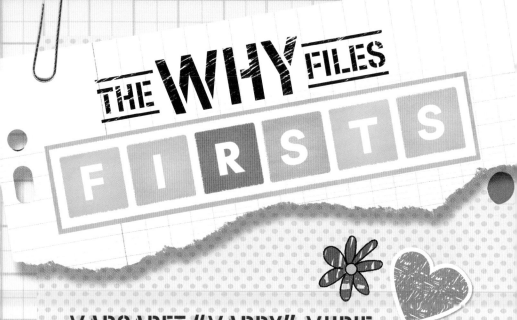

MARGARET "MARDY" MURIE

(1902–2003) was one of the first women conservationists of modern times. In 1964, she helped pass the Wilderness Act, which protects wildlands from destruction and preserves natural resources throughout the United States.

WANGARI MAATHAI (1940–2011) was a

Kenyan environmentalist who worked to protect trees, an important natural resource. She founded the Green Belt Movement to promote planting trees across Kenya. She was the first African woman to receive the Nobel Peace Prize.

LISA P. JACKSON (b. 1962)

is the first Black American to serve as the head of the United States Environmental Protection Agency (EPA). The EPA is a government agency that works to protect the environment and human health from pollution.

DORCETA TAYLOR (b. 1957)

is the first Black American woman to receive a doctoral degree from Yale University's School of the Environment. She works to make sure that people from diverse backgrounds have equal voices as we figure out the best ways to address issues that impact our environment.

I have MORE QUESTIONS now than I did before.

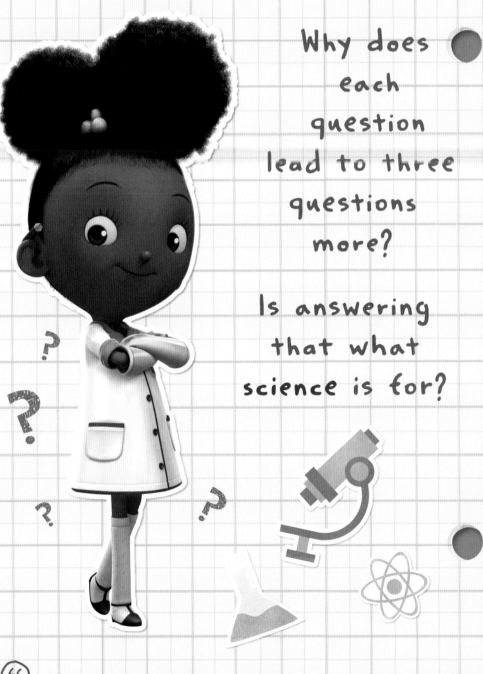

Why does each question lead to three questions more?

Is answering that what science is for?

MY QUESTIONS!

How much plastic waste do I create in one year?

How can I make less waste?

How do plants capture the Sun's energy?

How long does it take for sunlight to reach Earth?

Can we remove plastic waste from the oceans?

If people can use fewer resources, can whole towns do that, too? Can countries? Can companies? Can families?

How does a windmill work?

How hot is the Sun?

What is the strongest wind that ever blew on Earth?

Can we run out of water if the oceans are full of it?

How hot is Earth's core?

Are there undiscovered sources of energy out there?

SIMPLE

SCIENCE

EXPERIMENTS

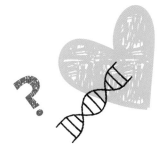

You can ask a grown-up for help!

BUILD A SOLAR STILL!

When waste gets into our water supply, the water becomes polluted, and we cannot use it. You can use the Sun's renewable energy to purify polluted water!

MATERIALS

- Large container to hold the polluted water (it should be large enough to hold a smaller container)

- Smaller container to collect purified water (make sure the smaller container will fit into the large one with some room to spare on the top and sides)

- 1 cup of water

- Food coloring

- Heavy item (like a paperweight) to weigh down the smaller container (if needed)

- Piece of clear plastic wrap, spare tarp, or tin foil (big enough to cover your large container)

- Rubber band (or adhesive tape)

- Small rock

INSTRUCTIONS

1 Fill the large container with water, about 1 inch deep. Add a few drops of food coloring to the water. (The food coloring will represent waste polluting the water.)

2 Place the smaller empty container in the middle of the large container. If the smaller container begins to float, put the heavy item inside of it to weigh it down. Be careful to make sure that none of the colored water gets inside the smaller container.

3 Place a piece of plastic wrap, tarp, or foil on top of the large container. Make sure the entire top is covered. The covering should be longer and wider than the top of the large container so that everything can be tightly sealed.

4 Use a rubber band to secure the covering in place around the rim of the large container. (Tape may work better for very large containers.)

5 Place a rock in the center of the covering, directly over the smaller container. This creates a dip that will cause water droplets to collect on the plastic wrap, tarp, or foil.

6 Place the solar still outside in a very sunny spot.

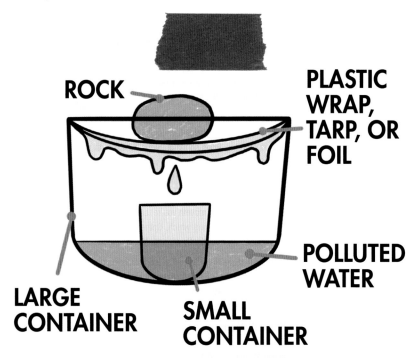

ROCK

PLASTIC WRAP, TARP, OR FOIL

POLLUTED WATER

LARGE CONTAINER

SMALL CONTAINER

7 Observe your solar still filtration system throughout the day to see how much water is collecting in the smaller container. You can leave the still outside for many days—this will allow the Sun to work its magic!

Using the power of the Sun, the water will be purified! Your smaller container should slowly fill with clean drinking water that does not have any food coloring in it. Cool, right?

Share your solar still on social media using #whyfileswonders!

BUILD YOUR OWN WIND TURBINE!

MATERIALS

- 7 wooden skewers
- 6 cardboard strips that are 6 inches long and 3–4 inches wide
- Packaging tape
- 1 cork
- Scissors
- 1 straw (preferably plastic-free)
- String
- Clean upcycled yogurt or pudding cup
- Empty cardboard paper towel roll

INSTRUCTIONS

1. Tape 6 skewers to cardboard strips: The flat part of the skewer should line up with the top of the strip. Leave about a 1-inch overhang on the spike end of the skewer. These are the blades.

2 Stick the pointy end of each blade skewer into the cork, spacing them evenly around the cork's side. Like this:

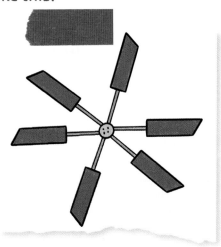

3 Take the final skewer and poke it into the end of the cork.

4 Cut the straw so that it is about half as long as the portion of the skewer sticking out of the end of the cork. Thread it on to the skewer. Like this:

5 Use tape to attach the cup to the bottom of the paper towel roll.

6 At the top of the roll, tape on the straw with the cork and blades facing out.

7 Take your wind turbine outside, and watch the wind rotate the blades!

8 Experiment! Create wind turbines with blades of different shapes, sizes, or materials, and see which work best!

Share your wind turbines on social media using #whyfileswonders!

Andrea Beaty

is the bestselling author of
the Questioneers series
and many other books. She
has degrees in biology and
computer science. Andrea
lives outside Chicago where
she writes books for kids and
plants flowers for birds, bees,
and bugs. Learn more about
her books at AndreaBeaty.com.

Sirk Productions

Theanne Griffith, PhD,

is a brain scientist by day and a
storyteller by night. She is
the lead investigator of a
neuroscience laboratory at
the University of California–
Davis and author of the
science adventure series the
Magnificent Makers. She lives
in Northern California with
her family. Learn more about
her STEM-themed books at
TheanneGriffith.com.

Samantha Jovan Photography

CHECK OUT THESE OTHER BOOKS STARRING
ADA TWIST, SCIENTIST

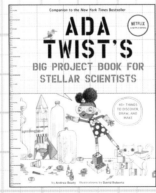

There's more to discover at **Questioneers.com**.